MACKENZIE'S LAST FIGHT WITH THE CHEYENNES

A Winter Campaign in Wyoming and Montana

By

CAPTAIN JOHN G. BOURKE, U.S.A.

1890

COPYRIGHT 2015 BIG BYTE BOOKS

Discover more lost history from BIG BYTE BOOKS

PUBLISHER'S NOTES

This book by the eminent soldier-scholar, John Bourke, is not really about the highly-regarded commander, General Ranald MacKenzie. It is a brilliant account of that general's last campaign; a campaign forgotten by most Americans but extremely important as a catalyst to ending the Great Sioux War of 1876.

Ranald MacKenzie (July 27, 1840–January 19, 1889) was considered, by none other than Ulysses S. Grant, at the end of the Civil War to be the most promising young officer in the United States Army. He had served in the battles of Second Bull Run, Antietam, Gettysburg, and through the Overland Campaign and Petersburg in 1864.

After the war he served the rest of his career on the western frontier. He was colonel of the 41st U.S. Infantry, a regiment of Buffalo Soldiers (African-American troops) in 1867. He participated in the Red River War and his command of the fight that defeated Dull Knife is detailed below.

In the early 1880's, a fall from a wagon caused a severe brain injury to MacKenzie. He soon began exhibiting bizarre behavior and was retired from service. He died at his sister's home in New York.

John Bourke's contribution to the history of the so-called Indian Wars cannot be overestimated. It is not as a soldier that he is best remembered, but as an anthropologist, ethnologist, folklorist, scientist, and writer—amazing for a man who was in uniform from the ages of 16 to 50. He kept regular journals throughout his time in the West and used them for this and other works, including his ethnographic work on Native American rites and his wonderful *On the Border with Crook*.

John Gregory Bourke was born on June 23, 1846 to Irish immigrant parents. His parents made sure he had an extensive early education that included studies of Latin, Greek, and Gaelic. He was just shy of fifteen when the Civil War broke out. The next year he ran away from home, lied about being 19, and entered service in the war. He was a Medal of Honor recipient for "gallantry in action" at the Battle of Stones River (December 31, 1862, to January 2, 1863), and also fought at Chickamauga. At the close of the war Bourke spent three months as private secretary to Secretary of War Edwin Stanton. Bourke's commander, General George Thomas ("the Rock of Chickamauga") later nominated him to West Point, where he also taught French; he graduated in 1869.

In 1881 he reported in writing to Lieutenant General Phil Sheridan on investigations he had made under special orders on Indian dances. He wrote and presented many papers, including "Mexican Cooking and Mexican Foods," which typically for Bourke contained much cultural information as well.

Bourke's major scholarly work was *Scatalogic Rites of All Nations. A Dissertation upon the Employment of Excrementicious Remedial Agents in Religion, Therapeutics, Divination, Witch-Craft, Love-Philters, etc. in all parts of the Globe.* A 1913 posthumous reprint contained a preface by none other than Sigmund Freud.

In 1883, Bourke married Mary F. Horbach, with whom he had three daughters. In 1896 he began treatment for an abdominal tumor related to a longstanding illness. He died at the Polyclinic Hospital in Philadelphia (his home state) on June 8, 1896 after a few weeks of treatment, just fifteen days shy of his fiftieth birthday. His wife was with him at the time.

You have in your hands one of the most important works on the period of the Indian Wars. It provides a perspective that too few in power at the time appreciated. Like many soldiers of the period, Bourke felt that the bloodshed and misunderstanding between whites and Indians was exacerbated and extended because of policies designed more for facilitating westward expansion than dealing fairly with native peoples. Though a serious topic that the author does nothing to minimize, he will make you laugh along the way.

BIG BYTE BOOKS

2015

MACKENZIE'S LAST FIGHT

IT may be a matter of interest to many readers to learn something of one of the most decisive encounters with bold and daring savages in which the soldiers of the Regular Army have ever been engaged; one in which the fierce, brave Cheyennes were humbled and their power shattered.

To avoid prolixity, and at the same time to present all that may be essential to a clear understanding of the situation, it is proper to say that in the war which began in the winter of 1876 between the United States Government on the one hand and the two tribes claiming an interest in the possession of the Black Hills of Dakota, on the other, the Cheyennes had been the more determined, more fierce and more resolute, although the Sioux furnished by far the stronger contingent, numerically considered, of the forces arrayed in hostility.

The operations begun in February, 1876, by the attack made by General Crook's forces upon the village of the Sioux chief, "Crazy Horse," on Powder River, Montana, and maintained throughout the ensuing summer and fall, by various large commands under [Generals] Crook, Terry, Gibbon, Miles and others, had not been specially fruitful in satisfactory results. To be candid, in not a few points of view, the hostile Indians had had much the best of the argument. Custer's command had been destroyed, or paralyzed, and the engagements of the Lower Powder, Tongue, Rosebud, Little Big Horn, Goose Creek, and Slim Buttes, had at first view not been decisive. But a second examination would discover that the lines of destiny were drawing tightly about the doomed aborigines. Their supply of ammunition, formerly almost limitless, was now absolutely cut off. Their friends and supporters en the Reservation were cowed into good behavior by the presence of large bodies of troops at the Agencies, by whom discipline was enforced of a stern, but just and salutary nature. "Red Cloud" and "Red Leaf," prominent Sioux chiefs, who, during the summer, had made no concealment of sympathy with their brethren on the war-path with "Crazy Horse" and "Sitting Bull," had been surrounded at the early dawn of a frosty October morning, all in their camps made prisoners, and every pony belonging to them seized and driven away.

Baffled and humiliated, they sulked in impotent rage, while the element in the tribe antagonistic to them gathered round the astute "Spotted Tail," listened to the counsels of General Crook and promised obedience and assistance to the Government whose rations they were eating. They kept their promises to the fullest extent. Hundreds of young warriors enlisted as scouts, and when in the latter part of October, 1876, the different portions of our command were ordered to rendezvous at Fort Fetterman, Wyoming, every Indian on the Reservation, or on the war-path, and every officer and soldier knew that the end was nigh.

From the official description of Fort Fetterman the reader can see that, in the days of which I am writing, it was situated in latitude 420 49' 8" North, longitude 105° 27' 3" West from Greenwich, on the south side of the North Platte River at its junction with La Prele (or Rush) creek. It was first established in July, 1867. The nearest stations on the Union Pacific Railway (Medicine Bow and Rock Creek), were eighty miles distant to the south, but as this "short" road was blocked with snow for nearly half the year, travel in the winter months followed the longer road to Cheyenne, 160 miles to the south-east, via Fort Laramie.

It contained quarters for three hundred enlisted men, and the necessary officers; the various magazines and store-houses required for the preservation of ammunition, rations and other supplies; a hospital with fifteen beds; stables for fifty horses; a corral capable of holding fifty six-mule wagons, with their animals; a theatre, an ice-house, a root-house, a granary, a bakehouse, blacksmith shops, saw-mill, saddlers' shop, paint shop, laundresses' quarters and a steam engine for pumping water from the North Platte River.

Any ordinary map will show at a glance exactly where Fort Fetterman was, the different roads by which the columns converged to that point, and the important part a military post played on the frontier.

The buildings had no pretensions to architectural elegance, being a single story each, of adobe, fronted by a veranda, but they served their purpose, were kept in good repair, were neatly painted and acted in a mild kind of a way as a Mecca for the first glimpse of which many a weary eye had strained its glance across the interminable plains between the Laramie and the Big Horn.

The expedition was composed of eleven companies of cavalry, from the 2d, 3d, 4th and 5th regiments, under command of General Ranald S. Mackenzie; four companies of the 4th Artillery, dismounted, and eleven companies of infantry, from the 4th, 9th, 14th and 25th regiments, under Colonel R. I. Dodge: the whole under the personal orders and supervision of Major-General George Crook.

Mackenzie, to whom the cavalry arm of the expedition had been assigned, was looked upon by the whole army as the embodiment of courage, skill and dash in an eminent degree. Impetuous, headstrong, perhaps a trifle rash, he formed a curious contrast to his self-poised, cool, silent commander whom the Indians of the plains and mountains from the British line to Mexico had learned to know and respect as the "Gray Fox."

Of the subordinate commanders and other officers, I cannot speak in detail; mention will be made of many in the appropriate places, but special reference in an article of this size and scope is impossible.

There was one comrade (much against his inclination, an absentee), of whom we often spoke kind words; Thaddeus H. Stanton, Colonel in the Pay Department, who had during previous campaigns handled the half-breed and full-blood auxiliaries, with courage, intelligence and skill. He never knew what it was to growl, never lost his temper, was at all times good-humored and helpful, full of story and reminiscence, a capital soldier, one of the best fellows in the Service, more like one of Charles O'Malley's dragoon companions than anyone I've ever met, but extremely modest in referring to his own hard service, which he seemed to think was a matter of course. I should like to mention, were it possible, the good qualities of every soldier: Words of praise from me to individuals, however, would scarcely be possible, but I can surely be permitted to laud them in the aggregate and say in words something like those of Tiny Tim: "God bless them, every one."

The total effective strength of the expedition was, in round numbers, fifteen hundred officers and men, including a medical staff of six surgeons. This was of white troops only; but our Indian auxiliaries, in whose praise too much cannot be said, aggregated not quite four hundred more, divided among Sioux, Arapahoes, Shoshonees, Bannocks, Pawnees, and, most important of all, a few friendly Cheyennes. The Crows in the Judith Basin, in northern Montana, sent word that two hundred of their best warriors would start under Major Randall, to combine with the expedition at or near Pumpkin Buttes, or old Fort Reno; "Spotted Tail" expressed his willingness to allow as many more of his young men to enlist, if required, and the Winnebagoes, friendly for many years, applied through their agent for permission to send a company to take part in the campaign.

The military plans may be outlined in one paragraph. With the Indian scouts scouring the country in front, flank and rear, no trouble was to be expected in locating the villages of the hostiles; then the cavalry under Mackenzie could be pushed forward to strike a sharp, decisive blow upon anything not beyond its ability to handle, or, failing in this, could fall back upon the infantry following more slowly in its trail. To supply a column of this size, in the depth of winter, was a problem demanding most careful consideration. There was a train of one hundred and sixty-eight wagons and seven ambulances, with two hundred and nineteen drivers and attendants; and a pack-train of four hundred mules cared for by sixty-five expert packers, to follow after the cavalry whenever it should cut loose from the main body.

No finer, cleaner-cut expedition was ever known in the annals of the Regular Army. A large percentage of the rank and file had been taught the stern lessons of Indian warfare in the movements of the two years preceding and could take care of themselves under any and all circumstances. Every man was provided with a fur cap, fur gloves, fur leggings and felt boots, or else the ordinary cavalry boot with Arctic "snow excluders." Three blankets were allowed each soldier, besides an overcoat and tentage (so long as with the wagon train).

Company K, 2d Cavalry, under the gallant "Teddy Egan," (long since dead) was detailed as Provost Guard at headquarters to supply mounted couriers and mail carriers when needed, attendants upon the "travois" carrying the wounded, and other valuable duties of a kindred type.

The Indian scouts were divided into detachments of suitable size, dependent upon tribal relations, commanded by Lieutenants William P. Clark, 2d Cavalry, W. S. Schuyler, 5th Cavalry, Hayden Delaney, 9th Infantry, and Major Frank North, the last named so well-known from his years of association with the Pawnees.

For more on the North brothers and their Pawnee battalion, see Two Great Scouts *by the eminent scholar, George Bird Grinnell.—Ed. 2015*

The Indian scouts were a superb lot of men, physically and mentally. Those who impressed me most were "Sharp Nose," chief of the Arapahoes, "Li-heris-oo-li-shar," or "Leading Chief," of the Pawnees, "Tupsi-paw" ("The Rag-picker") of the Shoshonees, and "Three Bears" of the Sioux; but in my long list of names, I discern those of such doughty warriors as "Pretty Voiced Bull," "Yellow Shirt," "Singing Bear," "Lone Feather," "Tall Wild Cat," "Black Mouse," "Charging Bear," "Feathers on the Head," "Fast Thunder," "Keeps the Battle," "Kills in the Winter," "Lone Dog," "No Neck," "Rocky Bear," "Six Feathers," "Sorrel Horse," "Horse Comes Last," "White Elk," "Bad Moccasin," "Fox Belly," and "Red Leaf."

Association with their white comrades soon begot a friendly intimacy under whose tender impulses names were exchanged, as in the case of Lieut. Charles Rockwell and others. Rockwell was our Commissary and a brighter or more efficient one never was known. The Indians saw plainly that a man who had absolute control over such immense quantities of bacon and sugar and coffee must rank very close up to the Great Father himself, so they made the friendliest overtures, offering to exchange not names alone, but clothes as well. Rockwell accepted the agnomen of "Six Feathers," but drew the line at the clothing business.

Only those who have known by actual experience, can appreciate the responsibility and labor entailed by the hurried organization of such an expedition, at any time and in any place, but more particularly when the time is an Arctic winter, and the place Fort Fetterman, Wyoming.

From the first sound of reveille in the morning until long after taps had hushed the worn-out troopers to rest, there was hurrying and scurrying worse than had ever been seen on Canoby Lea; all was movement, animation and activity. Heavily-laden wagons rumbled along the roadway or gathered in canvas-covered column, to discharge cargo or to reload at the Commissary; here and there stood the caparisoned horses of officers and orderlies, showing the location of the offices in which business was transacted. Sentinels paced with monotonous cadence their weary posts of duty; a battery of cannon, covered but not concealed by paulins, and the evening parade of the companies with their well-dressed alignment of disciplined stolidity were suggestions of military precision in high relief from the hurly-burly and apparent disorder surrounding them. Groups of blanketed, painted, savage allies gazed impassively on the treeless, ice-locked channel of the Platte.

Far away to the distant horizon, the white-mantled terraces, extended in ridge upon ridge until they touched the hems of the leaden robes of cloud the sky had just doffed. Flocculent masses of vapor, like Golden Fleeces in an ethereal Pactolus;—brilliant carmine and bronze patches straggling across the dome, catching the last reflections of the sun going down behind the Western mesas; amber tinted zones, interspersed with steely-blue stripes resting upon the receding strata of snow-clouds;—were negligently mingled in a combination of rare beauty; in whose contemplation the weariness of official routine was almost forgotten.

The sharp boom of the evening gun signalled the descent of the sun; slowly the golden tints of the clouds changed to bronze, to carmine, to a dull red; this last turned into a pale yellow blending imperceptibly into the darkness of night, relieved by myriads of sparkling stars.

The atmosphere in its purity gave free passage to every beam of light, or re-echoed the slightest sounds. Only the crunching of feet trampling the crisp, crystalline snow, or the barking of some shadow-scared hound, relieved the stillness. It was Night in Wyoming and Winter had begun.

At last all was ready: the last ration had been packed away, the last cartridge issued and stored in belt, the last mule shod. The last official communication had been written; the last report exacted by red tape had been consigned to the post-office for transmittal to the mausoleum in the pigeon-holes of the War Department. The last requisition had been signed, countersigned, or returned to be properly briefed. For the last time, weary and eyesore aides-de-camp had had the honor to acknowledge receipt of correspondence from Colonel A. and Major B. and Captain C., and to assure those estimable gentlemen that they were their very obedient servants; and for the last time the combined and pent-up ill-humor of the whole military establishment had burst with cyclonic wrath upon the devoted head of Major Furey, our efficient and amiable, that is usually amiable, quartermaster. He had been hauled over the coals by the general commanding, growled at by the battalion commanders, sneered at by the captains and damned by the lieutenants until patience had ceased to be a virtue and poor Furey assured me (during a lull in the storm of objurgation about midnight, while I was mixing him a little paregoric and hot water, or something like that—my notes are a trifle blurred at this point and I can't clearly make out what it was,) that if he ever lived through the campaign he intended to resign from the Service and set up in business as a pirate, anything, rather than be a quartermaster another day. However, he seems to have reconsidered this determination, for his name is still borne on the Register.

There were councils and councils, never-ending councils with the Indians, but even these too, had an end, and on the 14th of November, 1876, the old familiar road to Fort Reno stretched out in a long, snaky line over the low bluffs to the Northwest, as the column began picking its way through the floating ice across the North Platte.

The scene was certainly most picturesque and full of animation; everything moved like clock-work. Each man, horse, wagon and mule was in proper place and the crossing was effected without difficulty, the volume of water at that season being scant and the current sluggish, a pleasant variation from the turbid, swift-rolling torrent which had carried away the ferry-boat when the transfer was in progress the last spring and hurried several teamsters with their horses to graves beneath its waves.

From the North Platte crossing to the then remote outpost of Cantonment Reno on the Powder River at the foot of the Big Horn range, is not much over ninety miles and was made by easy marches in four days.

Of the intervening country, not a great deal can be said; it is "high-rolling mesa," fairly well grassed, with some cottonwood growing along the courses of the insignificant streams, which are not worth the trouble of a description. The water is frequently vile and is never good until you get up to the Piney, one of the forks of the Tongue, just beyond Reno, where trout may be found in considerable numbers and of good size.

Buffalo had formerly roamed over it, but in 1876, had retired over towards the Rosebud, a considerable distance to the West. Antelope were still to be found in great herds, and my notebooks recall to my recollection a very grand picture of a party of Indian scouts chasing a band of these fleet-footed coursers of the desert and shooting them down on the dead run.

So far the campaign had been without incident. There was nothing to talk about while marching and, even had there been, conversation would have flagged because your old soldier is a taciturn, grumpy animal on the march, not much given to an expression of opinion on any topic.

My personal inclinations led me to associate as much as possible with our savage scouts, whose modes of life, language and religious thought were always of an indescribable interest. Nearly all the talk I had with anybody was with them and the result was the enrichment of note-books with references to aboriginal customs in war and peace which probably could not have been obtained under circumstances of greater advantage. The American Indian is by nature so secretive and reticent that unless one by long personal association learns how to watch and extract information, much of what may be called his inner life, would inevitably be lost.

These Indian scouts covered the country for thirty to forty miles on each side of the column, letting nothing escape their scrutiny, but keeping their own movements well concealed. A party of them came upon three horse tracks shortly after we had left Sage Creek and followed them for a day, overtaking the riders, who proved to be white men, but whether pony thieves or "prospectors" they could not determine.

Part of the time we marched in the teeth of a biting storm of snow, and at every hour of the day the sun could be discerned sulking behind soft grey mists in company with rivals, known in the language of the plains as "Sun-dogs," whose parahelic splendors warned the traveller of the approach of the ever-to-be-dreaded "blizzard."

Cantonment Reno was not at that time suggestive of luxury or comfort: officers and men were living in holes excavated in the faces of clay-banks, or in make-shift quarters of similar type. It had been re-established for the protection of supplies to be issued to expeditions like our own, and answered its purpose well enough. The officers and soldiers of the garrison were taking things philosophically and there was no growling or complaint of any kind. Still, an order to report for duty at West Point, or New York, Fort Monroe or Washington would, I fancy, have been received with gladness and obeyed with alacrity by most of them.

More unaffected hospitality couldn't be found anywhere in the world. It's a very strange phenomenon in human nature that a lieutenant who has only two blankets, and neither of them any too good, will become fighting mad and want to shoot the visitor to his post who will not accept the use of one; but let the same fellow marry a rich girl and go to live in a "cottage" in Newport, with seventeen spare rooms to it, and his own brother may make himself as comfortable as he can in the gutter. It may be the fault of human nature, or it may be the fault of the girl; perhaps, of both, but it's a queer thing, anyway, and I, for one, can't understand it.

I anticipated a trifle when I spoke of the Shoshonee Indians being with the column, which they did not join until it reached Reno, where they were awaiting it, over one hundred strong, under command of Tom Cosgrove, an old acquaintance and an old frontiersman, and the sons of their head chief "Washakie."

We remained at Reno only long enough to let the blizzard expend its fury; the days were not wasted, however. The commanding general (Crook) assembled all his Indians and laid down to them, in a few well-chosen words, rules for their guidance during the campaign. He emphasized the fact that all these vast plains, all these mountains and valleys would soon be filled with a pushing, hard-working population, the game would be exterminated, domestic cattle would take its place, and the Indian must make up his mind, and make it up now, to live like the white man and at peace with him, or be wiped off the face of the earth. Peace, the white man wanted. War he was prepared for. He wanted to impress upon his hearers the great fact that law was not tyranny; people who obeyed the laws were those who had the largest amount of liberty. It was not the white man, but the Indian who was afraid when he went to sleep at night that he and all his family might be murdered before morning by some prowling enemy. They were going to get good pay as soldiers, and so long as they behaved themselves, and so long as he could find work for them to do, they should be soldiers, but they must not spend their pay foolishly. Save every cent of it and buy cows and mares. While the Indian was sleeping the calves and colts would be growing and someday he'd wake up and find himself a very rich man and then he'd be ashamed to call upon the Great Father for help. At this talk he saw before him representatives of the Kiowas, Blackfeet, Nez Perces, Cheyennes, Sioux, Arapahoes, Pawnees, Utes, Shoshonees, and Bannocks. What he said applied to them all. This was a good time to bury the hatchet and reconcile petty differences. Indians should be friendly to each other as well as the white man.

One word more. When they came upon a village of the hostile Indians they must be careful not to kill women or children, as he was determined to make an example of anyone caught disobeying this order.

The Indians listened attentively, and as sentence by sentence these remarks were translated by the interpreters or expressed in the sign-language, a chorus of Ughs! and grunts of approval passed from the inner circles to the outer. The greater portion of the Indians appeared in their new uniforms, yet a few sported magnificent war-bonnets of feather-work and other regalia. Responsive remarks were made by "Tup-si-paw" and "O-ho-a-tay" for the Bannocks and Shoshonees, "Sharp Nose" for the Arapahoes, "Three Bears" for the Sioux, and "Li-heris-oo-li-shar" and "U-sanky-su-cola" for the Pawnees.

"Li-heris-oo-li-shar" ("Leading Chief"), of the Pawnees, was determined to make the most of the occasion and impress upon the other Indians that he was nothing more or less than a white man, determined to "follow the white man's road."

The hand was the hand of Esau, but the voice was the voice of Jacob; his clothes were all right, a suit of Chatham Street "hand-me-downs" obtained from the munificence of the Interior Department during a visit to Washington; his face-painting, however, would not be justified by any of the canons of good taste inculcated by Ruskin or Whistler. Eye-lids and ears, and the median line of forehead and chin, blushed with vermilion; the cheek-bones were stained a dark brown, and the lower half of the face a dirty lemon. The hair was divided into two pigtails, wrapped in yellow tape and hanging over the ears.

That night (November 19, 1876,) a degraded wretch was caught selling whiskey to soldiers and Indians; his cart was confiscated and the heads of his barrels knocked in—a punishment utterly inadequate, as we were obliged the next day to consign to the grave a poor recruit who, under the influence of this vile liquor had wandered off in the snowy blast and frozen to death.

While the storm was at its worst, a detachment of Indian scouts, fourteen in number, (eight Arapahoes and six Sioux) were dispatched on a reconnoissance in the foot-hills of the Big Horn to the West.

The storm abated somewhat before day-break, but all of November 20th there were rough, cold gusts of wind from the north and north-west and occasional "flurries" of snow, but not enough to prevent our red-skinned auxiliaries from holding a delightful series of peace-talks, smokes and dances, in which there was mutual serenading, plenty in quantity, wretched in quality, some present-giving and protestations innumerable of the most affectionate friendship. Had I space, I could fill pages with descriptions of the curious customs brought out on these occasions, and will at an early day crave the attention of my readers while I relate them, but just now we must hurry on to other scenes.

Thirty-four miners from Montana reached Cantonment that day. They were almost starved and had narrowly escaped death in the blizzard. Rations were supplied them and all that the means at hand would permit was done for their comfort.

The reconnoitering party of fourteen Indian scouts whose departure was recorded a day or two back, returned, bringing with them a prisoner, a young Cheyenne warrior, who, seeing them dressed as his own people (they had taken the precaution to leave all military trappings behind), had mistrusted nothing until they had seized and bound him and started back on their long, cold ride of fifty miles to rejoin the main column. He was taken to headquarters, where cross-examination elicited the fact that he was one of a small party living in five lodges near the head of the Crazy Woman's Fork and that if they became alarmed, as they might by his failure to return, they'd surely break across the country to join "Crazy Horse," who was encamped close to our battle-field of the previous June, on the Rosebud, Montana.

General George Crook and his forces were attacked on June 17, 1876 by 1,500-2,000 warriors under Crazy Horse at the Battle of the Rosebud. Just eight days later, the same warriors were among those who destroyed five companies of troopers under George Armstrong Custer at the Little

Bighorn. The Rosebud fight was every bit as important a fight for both sides but is now forgotten by most, due to the death of the famous Custer on June 25.—Ed. 2015

The blizzard resumed its fury and the ground this night was covered deep with snow. We didn't mind that much, looking upon it as a benefit rather than a misfortune, because it would give all the better chance of drawing close to the enemy without discovery.

We were to start in the morning, prompt and early, so all hands were busy in scratching off a line to some of the folks at home: the mail was soon ready, and with the dispatches of the only correspondent who succeeded in catching the command before it started from the railroad—Mr. Roche, of the New York *Herald*—a companionable, scholarly gentleman, who has since abandoned journalism and become possessed of considerable means in Texas—was securely wrapped and tied in an oil-silk envelope and given to the courier, whose prompt, hearty "Good night, gentlemen," was uttered at the same instant with pull of rein and dash of spur—and in a moment more, he had disappeared in the gloom, to fight his way, as best he might, through snow and sleet, cold and danger of all kinds, back to Fort Fetterman, ninety miles.

A few remarks touching the principal Indian chief accompanying us may be of value.

"Sharp Nose," of the Arapahoes, was tall, straight, of large frame, with piercing eyes, Roman nose, firm jaws and chin and a face inspiring confidence in his ability and determination. His manners were dignified and commanding, coming nearer to the Fenimore Cooper style of Indian than any I had seen since my visit to "Cocheis," the renowned chief of the Chiricahua Apaches, in the Dragoon Mountains, Arizona, in February, 1873.

"Li-heris-oo-li-shar," the Pawnee, had a good face, prominent cheek bones, aquiline nose, large mouth and frank, open eyes, not so piercing as those usually to be noticed among the aborigines. He had the air of a far-seeing, judicious law-giver, one who took note of all he saw and whose advice could be relied on. Yet, he was no lamb, as the outlines of his countenance plainly showed that, if aroused, he would be a bad enemy.

"Tupsi-paw" and "O-ho-a-tay," of the Shoshonees, were crafty old rascals, without much sentiment or romantic imagination lighting up their features.

"Three Bears," of the Sioux, was young in years, but mature in thought. He looked, as he was, a man whose friendship could be relied on. He made no pretensions as a speaker and cut but a poor figure in declamation, when "Sharp Nose" was in the same council. His power as a commander depended more upon the success to be won from stealthy movements and crafty combinations than from any lion-like attack such as "Sharp Nose's" face suggested he might make.

On Wednesday, November 22d, 1876, we moved to the Crazy Woman's Fork of Powder River, about twenty-five miles from Cantonment Reno; on the banks of that stream at a point where good water, grass and fuel were to be had in abundance, and where an extended view of the surrounding country made surprise difficult, the supply train of wagons was ordered to park and remain, with a strong guard, under Major Furey, the quartermaster. Ten days rations were packed on mules, one hundred rounds of ammunition issued to each man, and all preparations made for swinging loose for a march in search of "Crazy Horse's" village.

During this afternoon, the Indian scouts killed three buffaloes and brought the meat back to camp; this wasn't, by any means, the last time that I saw buffalo on the plains, but I make allusion to the fact as the great herds have now entirely disappeared.

I have just said that General Crook's intention had been to push out from the "Crazy Woman" and strike the camp of the great Sioux chief "Crazy Horse," believed to be then on the upper Rosebud, Montana, near our old battle-field of the previous June. This plan was changed by a trifling circumstance.

Shortly after dawn on the morning of November 23d, a white flag waved from the crest of a bluff in the vicinity of our camp. It was borne by "Sitting Bear," a Cheyenne Indian, who had been dispatched from Red Cloud Agency by Col. J. W. Mason, in advance of the expedition, to bear an ultimatum to the hostiles and ask them to surrender without bloodshed. He was soon at headquarters, with the important information that the capture of the young Cheyenne warrior had alarmed his village, which had started across the hills to join "Crazy Horse." There was, however, he understood, another Cheyenne village, an extremely large one, hidden in the cañons of the Big Horse range near the sources of the "Crazy Woman" the very stream we were on.

To determine the location of this village, to surprise and destroy it, was, in one word, the order of the day. General Mackenzie was ordered to take the Indian scouts and all the cavalry, but one company, and push up the "Crazy Woman's" Fork to its head, and then strike in to the Big Horn mountains and hunt for what fate might have in store for him. All told, Mackenzie had an effective force of exactly eleven hundred officers and men, one-third of the number being Indian scouts. The infantry and artillery companies, and one company of cavalry, the last reserved for employment as couriers and mounted work generally, were to follow as promptly as possible on the trail of the first division.

Preceding all, by eight or ten miles of distance, was a very small detachment of Indian scouts, selected with special reference to their knowledge of this particular section of country, coolness, good judgment and experience in war.

There are few sights more inspiring to a military observer than a compact, well-disciplined column of cavalry, "fined down" to a minimum of impedimenta, moving rapidly, silently and with malice aforethought along the trail of an enemy. Especially is such the case when the march is made in the depth of winter, in a flurry of snow, by day or by night, when the fur-clad veterans, gleaming from head to foot in an additional coating of crystal rime, and with heavy beards matted with the ice of frozen breaths, bring back to recollection all the childhood legends of Santa Claus and Jack Frost.

Closing well up on the rear of the column followed the pack-train, each mule and packer selected after an examination alongside of which the severest tests of our much-vaunted civil service seem trivial; but an examination whose rigor will commend itself to all who reflect that upon the absolute, undoubted efficiency of every man and mule depends the celerity and promptness with which the ammunition, rations and blankets of the command are to reach camp each night.

No officer of the United States Army has given the earnest, intelligent attention to the subject of pack-mule transportation as has General Crook; he may, without qualification, be called the apostle of the military pack-train. He recognized the importance of this branch of study, made it his own from Alpha to Omega, introduced military promptness and discipline into the system already prevailing, and had the gratification of seeing his severe labor rewarded by the success attending his campaigning in the mountains and on the plains. There is not a pack-train in the Army to-day which does not trace back its first organization to General Crook in Arizona in 1871, although many years prior to that he had run others on the same principles in Oregon and California.

In his official report of the disaster at the Little Bighorn, General Alfred Terry noted that his Dakota column, including the 7th United States Cavalry under Custer, were not accustomed to using pack animals. The pack train that Custer took up the Rosebud and into the Little Bighorn Valley consisted of mules taken from the wagon train; animals that were not trained to carry aparejo packs. When Custer's men went into the fight, the pack train was miles behind them.—Ed. 2015

I don't wish to travel out of my way into a dissertation upon pack-trains and their management; I will introduce only one remark to show with what care a first-class "train" must be organized. No mule, if such a thing can be avoided, will be accepted by a train-master of experience, when the mouth shows signs of "bridle-wear"—that is, evidence of the animal having been so long used in harness that the constant tugging and pulling on the bridle have worn out the lips at their point of juncture.

The explanation given for this is easy enough to understand. Such an animal cannot slake its thirst half so readily as one whose mouth has not been injured, because much of the water it may take into its mouth while crossing a stream will escape at the sides. Time is nowhere so important an element as on military forced marches: the old pack-master knows that as well as does the oldest general, and therefore rejects, whenever he can, mules of the class I speak of.

The muleteers themselves must be strong, lithe, active, not afraid of hard work, and willing to take cheerfully the roughest kind of knocks. The pack-train is, from first to last, an exotic, imported in the early days of California mining from the Andean slopes of Chile and Peru; the packers whom I met in my first years of service were, with scarcely exceptions enough to emphasize the rule, natives of the two countries named, or of the western States of-Mexico. They were a good-natured, merry-hearted set of fellows, ever anxious to render kind services and delighted beyond expression when they happened to run across an officer desirous of jotting down the tender words of their dainty Spanish songs of love disdained and unrequited. To form an opinion from the theme of almost every one of these amorous ditties, the Cavalier of Castilian origin would appear to be an individual of charming qualities of mind and person—one to whose pleadings the proudest and noblest lady should be glad to listen. His voice, his music, his earnest devotion, all, are thrown away upon the dark eyed witch who lurks in the immediate vicinity of the lattice overlooking his position, but who deigns no sign of acquiescence or approbation. It may be a trifle late in the day for me, a foreigner, to express a withering contempt for this much lauded beauty, insensible to music of an entrancing type, and the occasion, I am certain, of many grievous cases of pneumonia and pleurisy, originating in the exposure of these serenades. I have waited for years, hoping to learn that she had something to say for herself, that there was a woman's side to this distressing story. None has come. All Spanish love-songs point the one moral, and I am, consequently, much against my will, forced to the conclusion that the Spanish lover is a greatly abused individual whom I advise to turn his back upon the stony-hearted maidens of his fatherland and come to our own glorious country, where the sex is not so refractory.

The first-class packer was, invariably, I might say, a first-class cook, to whose courtesy and forethought I have been on many a cold, chilly night indebted for an invigorating cup of chocolate, or nourishing plate of "frijoles," dishes which are utterly beyond the grasp of our boasted American civilization.

The American is equalled by no people in the world for his ability to comprehend questions of constitutional law, to lay and construct railroads and to organize and manage, sometimes to wreck, great banking institutions; but when it comes to the business of catering to the inner man, he is as stupid and helpless as a baby. Were I to be called upon this moment to choose between a cup of chocolate and a plate of beans prepared by my old friends "Chileno John," or "Lauriano Gomez," and the same viands concocted by Jay Gould or Leland Stanford, I know what my decision would be.

Being indirectly of Spanish origin, it was to be expected that many of the terms used in pack-trains should betray their derivation. This was the case and has only begun to change with very recent years; the words "*acemila*" for "pack-mule," "macho," used almost in the same sense, "*sencero*" for "bell-mare," "*atajo*" for the pack-train itself, "cargo" for the load each animal was to bear, and "*cargador*" for the official whose duty it was to arrange and distribute these burdens, were as well understood by officers of the Army serving in Arizona and New Mexico in the decade from 1865 to 1875 as their English equivalents.

And this philological survival has an interesting historical significance. Often as I trudged alongside of the pack-trains and listened to "Long Jim" Cook, or "Jim O'Neil," or Tom Moore, or "Hank'n Yank," or some other American overseer or pack-master, as "he his descant wildly thus began," upon the merits of "that thar puss mule," or "you, Keno! you, Billy! g'lang thar," my mind would insensibly revert to the descriptions of the Siege of Grenada, wither Isabella the Catholic ordered the removal of her Court to the newly-erected city of the Holy Faith and brought together more than 15,000 mules to carry rations to her followers.

Every man keeps concealed in his inner heart a small but carefully selected package of vain regrets, which he takes out from time to time, looks over carefully, and puts back in the arcanum. One of mine, I may here confess, has been the lack of occasion for stringing together all the incidents and adventures, buried in my note-books, in which appear the names of my warm friends, Tom Moore, Jim O'Neil, Hank'n Yank, Delaney, Young, Harry Hawes, Frank Monach, Daily, "Long Jim" Cook and "Short Jim" Cook, Charlie Hopkins, "Lauriano," "Chileno John," Josd de Leon, Vasquez, Castro, and dozens of other packers; Frank Gruard, Ben Clarke, Al. Seiber, "Big Bat" and "Little Bat" (i. e., Baptiste Pourrier and Baptiste Changrau), Ben Roland, Frank North, Tom Cosgrove, Jack Crawford, and scores of white scouts and guides, not to mention those of purely aboriginal blood.

"Buffalo Bill" Cody and his devoted friend and servant, "Buffalo Chips" White, appear time and again in my pages, always at the front of danger; the former is now too well-known to need a word of praise from me, and the latter, poor fellow, sleeps where he fell, not many feet from my side, in the fight at Slim Buttes, Dakota, September 9th, 1876.

My readers will kindly bear with me, I hope, for bringing in with special particularization old "Uncle Dick" Kloster, one of the pack-train veterans now dead and gone. As he presents himself to my recollection, he is clad from head to heel in fur and blanket-lined canvas, a musk-rat cap upon his head, while from eyes to breast depends a snow-white beard, matted like a board with frozen tobacco juice, because it was during the severe privations we underwent together in the campaign in Montana in the early months of 1876, when we were marching on half-rations, with the mercury frozen solid in the thermometer. Every afternoon, the moment the column made camp, out came my note-books, and the events of the day were recorded; in ink, until the severe cold broke the bottle and afterwards, as well as numbed fingers would permit, in lead pencil.

"Uncle Dick" would first look after his mules and then hurry to my side, doing everything in his power to add to my comfort. Sometimes, he would pile up "aparejos" (a form of pack-saddle) to keep the fierce north wind from carrying me away bodily; sometimes, build a fire at my feet, to keep my toes from freezing, but always something.

At last he unbosomed himself. He believed I was going to write a book, "as big as that thar Webster's Dictionary I seed down to Luke

Murrin's s'loon in Shy-an;" no man could be taking all those notes for nothing, and poor "Uncle Dick," like many of better education, mixed up the two ideas of quantity and quality. He had been on the Pacific Slope, in the Rocky Mountains, in British America and in Mexico, since 1849, had had his own share of "ups and downs," but had never yet "seed" his name in print. Could I—would I—put his name in "the" book?

When I told the dear old soul that not his name alone, but a full reference to his valuable kindness as well, should appear in a prominent page, the smile that spread over his face cracked the frost on his beard. "Look, Uncle Dick, here's your name, see for yourself." This recognition roused his generous good nature to a paroxysm of enthusiasm; he multiplied his efforts and ventured every now and then to proffer bits of information, some of it of consequence and some not, but all received most gratefully. I overheard him once confiding to an open-mouthed packer, that "me'n the Cap'n air gettin' up a book'bout Injuns'n mos' everythin'," and my last parting word from the old man was: "Cap, don't forgit that thar book outfit." No, Uncle Dick, I have not forgotten, and I hope you may be able to read these lines from the 'packer's' Paradise, to which I am sure you have gone, and where your honest old soul would be grieved did you not find an abundance of grass and water for your mules, no flies to bother them, and the very best of rations for your men—beans and bacon, "yeast powder" bread, dried apples, coffee and chocolate and an occasional "snootful" of something to drive away malaria.

Mackenzie and the cavalry made a rapid march of twelve miles or more up the "Crazy Woman," passing over as fine a pastoral region as is to be found in the world, and then, upon the advice of the Indian scouts, bivouacked in a spot well hidden among the foot-hills of the Big Horn range, to which we had been drawing closer and closer all afternoon. Colder and colder became the night, the stars glinted pitilessly from the inner depths of the blue ether which are hidden from Eastern eyes, but the feeling that we were sure to have a fight of some kind within possibly twenty-four hours, kept blood in circulation and when an electric pulsation of steely gray flashed upwards from the Eastern horizon to herald the near approach of the God of Day, not a man or horse showed the slightest bad effect of the Polar temperature, a fact I recorded with much pleasure in my notes at the time.

We resumed our march as soon as we could discern the trail of our advance detachment which led in towards the Big Horn mountains, going a trifle west of south, as it had on the previous day, and through much the same kind of fine grazing country. For about three hours we moved as rapidly as the frozen ground permitted; the slippery, frost-mantled grass offered no serious obstacle, but we did find all we could do to cross the innumerable "cut-bank" dry beds of streams, every one of which had to be broken down into suitable slopes by which the animals could descend and ascend. The ground was every bit as hard as flint and took up a great deal of valuable time before it would yield to axe or pick, which it frequently broke. Many of these crevices in the surface were not more than fifteen or twenty feet wide, so that the great labor involved in their passage had all the appearance of an unnecessary aggravation of our discomforts. We were growling and grumbling not a little at these troubles when the advance scouts rejoined at a run, and from head of column to rear guard spread the magnetic whisper that the enemy's village had been discovered and was almost under our noses. From the information brought in by the Indian scouts General Mackenzie concluded to halt just where we were until the rising of the moon, and then move slowly and cautiously forward to attack the enemy at daybreak. Our Indians had noted carefully every foot of the way, both going and returning, and knew exactly where to take us. Besides this, two of their number—"Red Shirt" and "Jackass"—had remained behind, hidden among the rocks on the top of a high hill from which coign of vantage everything transpiring in the village below was distinctly visible. I think it only fair to make special allusion to this act of daring and good judgment, for the very excellent reason that many inexperienced and unthinking persons, military as well as civil, have allowed themselves to be drawn into the error of disparaging and depreciating the services of Indian auxiliaries; on this, as on every other occasion of my twenty years close observation of them, they were of the greatest possible help to our soldiery, acting with the whites or singly. As already indicated, they represented on this campaign many different tribes, some of them being Cheyennes, closely related to the people we were soon to fight.

"Red Shirt" is, I think, the same Indian who has within the past year or two accompanied "Buffalo Bill" across the ocean and been presented to her Majesty, Queen Victoria.

There was no shouting, no cheering, no loud talking to show excitement; an old soldier would have known, however, that the news passing along so quietly and yet so swiftly from mouth to mouth was enough to set a civilian's blood on fire, he would have known it from the way men were looking at the fastenings of their saddle-girths and bridles, examining for the last time the action of breech-block and trigger, or making sure that no cartridge should be missing when wanted.

We didn't have very long to wait that short, hazy, bleak November day for the setting of the sun and the coming of our good friend, the moon. The grim bosom of the Big Horn Mountains parted to admit the column into a deep cañon whose vertical walls carved into turrets and battlements by the erosion of time and the elements, proclaimed almost with the eloquence of human tongue that those who entered must leave all hope behind.

Hidden by these lofty pinnacles, the coquettish moon played hide and seek, anon bathing the barrels of carbines and the metal work of bridles in an effulgence of light and again deserting us in darkness so opaque that the gentle glitter of kindly stars seemed to acquire the power of countless suns.

All night long we groped our way, floundering, slipping, struggling over smooth knolls of glassy surface, making the slowest kind of progress, but still advancing. Not a word was spoken above a whisper. Not a match was lighted, and the soldier's faithful friend, his pipe, was not allowed to leave the saddle-bags.

The most stringent orders were given that the column should keep "closed up," and each company as fast as it had worked its way across an unusually difficult ravine passed word to the front of its success and of the whereabouts of the company next behind it.

The Indian scouts manifested much greater anxiety than did their white brethren, probably because they understood the gravity of the situation better. They had calculated that the march to the hostile village could readily be made during the hours of night, but none knew better than they that there was not a moment to be wasted. If our attack could be made in the earliest hours of the morning, taking the enemy completely by surprise, the smaller loss should be on our side; should delays overtake us and the light of the coming day disclose our approach to vigilant and awakened savages, the percentage of loss upon which we might reasonably count was to be reckoned only by the amount of ammunition the hostile Cheyennes would have to expend in the contest.

So closely was our attention occupied by the task of working a way across the precipitous ravines which seamed and gashed the bottom of the cañon adown which rippled over its rocky bed the waters of the stream, called, as best we could determine, Willow Creek, and which on account of this same rippling were not frozen into solid ice—that our dull ears did not seize upon the ominous thumping of the Cheyenne war drums faithfully but feebly re-echoed by the towering walls which hemmed us in. Not so with the Indian scouts. Their faces might remain stolid and impassive, but every movement of muscle and sinew betrayed a frenzy of suppressed excitement.

One of them nudged me with his elbow and then pointed with his lips up the cañon in a way peculiar to savages. There was no doubt of his meaning; we were within rifle-shot of our quarry, but he wasn't asleep, as we had hoped to find him, but in full possession of his senses and dancing a great War-dance, in celebration of some recent victory. We threw ourselves on the ground and then heard with startling distinctness the thumping of the drums, the sleepy intonation of the tired out "medicine men" and warriors and the patter of languid feet. The dance was almost over, but the dawn had almost come.

2

THERE we lay, afraid to breathe lest a cough or a sneeze should betray our presence; dreading the impatient champing of tired and frozen horses, or the echo awakened by the falling upon the ground of the carbine of some clumsy soldier.

"Sharp Nose," the Arapahoe chief, with dilated nostrils and flashing eyes, moved nervously from point to point on his wiry pony, looking the incarnation of the Spirit of War.

All the discontent and disquietude engendered during that night of cold and anxiety came to a head at that moment; our eyes nervously scanned the battlements behind which hostile sharp-shooters might within the next few hours be taking position. It might be our misfortune to have to fight our way back—who could tell?

There came a low, Hist! from the front where the Indian scouts had massed, impatiently awaiting the signal to dash forward. It was not long in coming. The rearmost company was reported "up." Every man was in place, every horse was pressing on the bit. Anything was preferable to another moment of suspense; the noise of the Cheyenne drums had ceased and Gallop! was the order.

I heard nothing more—all was rush and clamor and shock, but the rush and clamor and shock of thoroughly organized, pitiless war.

It was the rush of a mighty river, the roar of a giant engine, but each drop of water knew its destined channel, each element of the machine knew the function it had to perform.

Back from the walls of the cañon, repeated fifty-fold by the echo, sounded the sharp words of command, the neighing and plunging of excited steeds, the clatter and clangor of arms, the ear-piercing shrieks and yells of savage allies, their blood-curdling war-songs, and the weird croon of the sacred flageolets of the Pawnee medicine men who, like the Celtic bards of old, rode boldly at the head of their people.

The Shoshonees and Bannocks followed Tom Cosgrove and Lieutenant Schuyler; Frank North led the Pawnees—these two detachments on the left and right flanks respectively, while down the centre thundered the solid column of Sioux, Cheyennes and Arapahoes, under Lieut. Philo Clark, a brave and brilliant cavalry officer, now dead, and Lieut. Hayden Delaney, who had faced the leaden tempests of twenty-eight pitched battles before he gained his cadetship, and yielded the palm of valor and coolness to no man in the Grand Old Army of the Tennessee, not even when U. S. Grant was its commander.

The cañon widened within a couple of hundred yards, forming an amphitheatre, giving room for our battalions to gallop front into line before sweeping across a small plateau alongside the village whose scores of lodges hugged the shelter of the stream-bed.

As our soldiers, red and white, rushed in at one end of the village, the frightened Cheyennes, tumbling half-naked from their beds, with nothing in their hands but rifles and belts of ammunition, were escaping from the other. In the exultation of the moment our people forgot the cold, the sleeplessness, the fatigue and hunger of the two previous days, and made the rocks resound with their cheers and shouts of derision. The Cheyennes answered never a word. They hurried women and children to places of comparative safety farther up the flanks of the mountains, and then crawling into sheltered nooks and crevices awakened the echoes with the sharp crack of rifles and the ominous ping of bullets, each seeking its billet. Under cover of this fire, they perfected arrangements for the safety of their households, but reserved further demonstrations until a few bold youngsters stealthily creeping back through the mist of early morning should have driven out of our clutches the herd of several thousands of ponies, hundreds of which were already enveloped by our lines. Several of their warriors had already been killed or wounded in an endeavor to save this precious stock, and I may say that one of the most vividly remembered episodes of the whole affair is the balking of my horse at the stark and stiffening body of a dying Cheyenne boy who lay directly across my path shot through the neck as he was bravely trying to stampede the ponies in the very teeth of our scouts. Wound loosely about his neck was his lariat; no doubt in my mind, that he had slept with it around or beside him, ready to spring out of his bed and rope the first pony he might run against in just such an emergency as this in which he had yielded up his young life to a sense of duty worthy of any Spartan.

But crawling in behind rocks and bluffs, dodging from tree to tree, and sneaking back among the tepis of the village itself, the bold, cunning Cheyennes were making ready to fight for their herds and drive us back down the cañon. The mist had lifted and the light of morning was filtering down into the cañon. The movements of the enemy were detected and General Mackenzie, realizing that not a moment was to be lost, ordered Lieut. John A. McKinney, with his company "M" of the 4th Cavalry to charge into the place where the enemy appeared to be concentrating. The brave young officer never faltered an instant, but charged across the plateau and down upon the Cheyennes, until he came to a gully with "cut" banks, which completely checked his advance. As his little command was wheeling by fours to the right to pass this obstacle, a small party of the hostile sharpshooters, concealed in and around the gully, and almost under our horses' bellies, opened a murderous fire, beneath which poor McKinney fell, struck by six bullets, six of his men wounded and a number of his horses shot. The company was thrown into confusion and several of the sets of fours turned in retreat. Mackenzie had observed the unfortunate turn of affairs and another company—that of Captain John M. Hamilton, 5th Cavalry, being at hand, he ordered it to the rescue, Major G. A. Gordon, 5th Cavalry, accompanying this charge with some men of the 4th and 5th not belonging to Hamilton.

The Cheyennes were unprepared for this second onslaught, which being most vigorously pressed, drove them back in confusion. Davis of the 4th Cavalry, coming up on Hamilton's flank followed in after the Cheyennes and boldly attacked them in the rocks and gullies where they tried to make a stand. This was the hottest part of the fight, and both Davis' and Hamilton's men had hand to hand fights with the savages; twenty of the bravest warriors of the Cheyennes bit the dust, and eight of their bodies fell into our hands. From all sides the enemy began closing in upon Davis, and would, I am certain, have wiped out both him and Hamilton, had it not been for the masterly judgment shown by Lieutenant Schuyler who had ordered his Shoshonee scouts to make their way to the summit of a very steep crag which commanded the village, the plateau and the whole position, and was, in fact, the key-point. The joyous yell of the

Shoshonees proved that they recognized the value of their success; half of them began a demoniacal dance of triumph to the music of the Cheyenne war-drum, captured on the ground where it lay just outside of the village; shrieks of joy almost drowned the roar of the volleys their more sagacious, but not a bit more blood-thirsty, comrades were pouring in upon the discomfited Cheyennes.

Mackenzie realized that the day was won, but he did not let the grass grow under his feet in taking every measure necessary to secure the fullest fruits of his victory. Hemphill of the 4th and Hamilton of the 5th, were ordered to seize and hold two high knolls on our right, and thus prevent any portion of the enemy from slipping in behind that flank and annoying us by a cross fire from the rear.

Captain A. B. Taylor and Lieutenant Wheeler, 5th Cavalry, made a gallant charge lengthwise through the village, forcing out the last lurking sharp-shooter and occupying the small fringe of timber just beyond the village, while Frank North and the Pawnees, darting in under cover of Taylor's movement, filled the village itself.

Russell and Wessells, with their companies of the 3d, covered the line between Hamilton and Taylor, while clusters of Arapahoe and Sioux marksmen held every clump of bushes, every projecting rock and every eminence along our whole front.

Three companies of the 4th, one of them McKinney's, were held in reserve behind protecting knolls, a short distance to the rear.

The day was won, and no one saw that better than did the Cheyennes. They could not retire from our immediate front with their women and children, because that would precipitate an attack and entail further loss. Their policy was to hold on to their natural fortifications in the high rocks, from which we could not dislodge them, until night-fall, and then withdraw with their families, their wounded and dead to some locality impregnable to assault.

Our men were peremptorily ordered to lie down under cover and to waste no ammunition. There were paroxysmal volleys from one side or the other, but the losses suffered were trifling, and so far as the Americans were concerned there was no great amount of danger, shelter being adequate, except in the cases of aides-de-camp, orderlies and officers reporting for instructions who, in moving from one flank to the other, if not able to hug the cover of a favorable ravine, were compelled to ride full tilt, exposed to a more than generous share of leaden attentions from Cheyenne sharp-shooters.

One of our soldiers met with death in a rather curious way. He disregarded his orders, and lifted his head and shoulders above cover. Hardly had he done so before a Cheyenne rifleman had drawn bead and put a bullet through his jaws; knocked senseless by the blow, he fell forward, but still remaining on his feet, against the bank in front of him. The blood from his wound poured down his throat and choked him to death. Had he fallen head downward, the blood would have flowed out from his mouth, and his life, perhaps, been saved, as the wound was not necessarily a fatal one.

To dispel the monotony, numbers of the Cheyennes rode out under the fire of our Shoshonees and others, hurled their contempt and defiance at them, and then returned to their own lines.

There was something peculiarly irritating in all this to the Shoshonees, between whom and the Cheyennes a special hatred seemed to exist. The cañon became a perfect bedlam with the echoing and re-echoing of rifle volleys and the yells and counter-yells of exasperated savages, but through it all the Cheyennes would dash about on their war-horses, chanting their songs, and bearing charmed lives whose frail thread the fickle Fates disdained to cut.

There was one notably daring warrior or chief, a powerful looking man, riding a fine white horse and himself bearing on his left arm a circular shield of buffalo hide and upon his head a war-bonnet, whose pendant eagle plumes swept the ground at his horse's feet. Bullets struck the ground before him, behind him, beside him; the air groaned with the ominous whistle of Death's messengers, but each and all spared the grim Cheyenne who serenely rode along the front of our line, venting derision in the teeth of his foes, until the cool, deadly aim of Lieutenant Allison, of the 2d Cavalry, knocked him lifeless from his charger.

Before the cheers from the whites and their Indian allies had died away, there issued from the Cheyenne line a young warrior gorgeous in his decorations of feathers, mounted upon a spirited pony, and bearing also upon his left arm a shield of buffalo hide, hardened in the fire and decorated with the plumage of the bald-headed eagle. This brave Cheyenne charged recklessly into the face of death, scorning the bullets which made the air hot about him, and chanting loudly the war-song proclaiming his determination to save from profane hands the corpse of his comrade and friend. On he flew, whipping into more energetic movement the faithful beast whose instinct warned it of imminent peril. Much sooner than it has taken to write this paragraph, he was bending over the bleeding form of the red-skinned Ajax, whose defiance was still sounding in our ears. Many were the expressions of admiration from our side as he lifted the body across the withers of the pony, and then springing lightly into the saddle, plied vigorously the quirt (or Indian whip of leather) and turned back to regain the friendly shelter of the rocks and gulches.

Escape seemed secure, but Fate was only mocking the poor wretch. In War, business is business, and bullets must fall upon the just and unjust, the cowardly and the brave.

Almost within hand-shake of his people, the heroic Cheyenne and his sturdy pony, freighted with so precious a burden, bore testimony to the precision of our marksmen, and fell pierced with many wounds. They had been comrades in battle and in campaign; and in death they were not divided. "Greater love than this hath no man than that he lay down his life for his friend."

The existence of this battle-comradeship among North-American tribes is a well-ascertained fact. The incident just described was one of many coming under my notice, not on this occasion alone, but at the fight on the Rosebud and elsewhere; it is more apparent, perhaps, among the Plains tribes, but can be found among the Bannocks and others on the west of the Rockies.

There was a lull in the action for a few moments to allow Bill Roland and a small party of half-breeds and Cheyenne scouts to crawl up closer to the enemy's position and begin a parley. At first the enemy were disinclined to a conference, and were more desirous of showering bullets than compliments upon their interrogators. Curiosity conquered antipathy, however, and enough of a conversation was had to let us know that "Dull Knife" and "Little Wolf" were the chiefs in command. The former, with two companions, approached near enough to let Roland know that he had had three sons killed in the fight and was personally willing to surrender, but unable to influence "Little Wolf," "Roman Nose," "Gray Head" and "Old Bear," who were all present with the village. These Indians called out to our Indian scouts: "Go home, you have no business here. We can whip the white soldiers alone, but can't fight you, too."

Then others of the hostile Cheyennes approaching, called out that they were going over to a big Sioux village they asserted to be nearby and get its assistance and come back and clean us out. "You have killed and hurt a heap of our people," they said, "you may as well stay now and kill the rest of us."

The talk of the Cheyennes was still fierce enough and their courage was unabated; had we foolishly attempted to force them out of their improvised rifle-pits in the crevices and behind the rocks on the hill sides, the loss of life would have been fearful. Prudence suggested that we make sure of what we had gained, move off all the herd of ponies rounded up by our Indian scouts, burn and destroy every vestige of the village, and send back to General Crook for the infantry with a view to having them bring their more powerful rifles to bear upon the hostiles in the morning in case they did not withdraw to another position during the darkness of night.

Our own losses were of course known: one commissioned officer (McKinney), six enlisted men killed; and twenty-six wounded. Thirty of the Cheyenne dead fell into our hands; sixteen scalps were taken, by Pawnees and Shoshonees; the other scouts did not take any, respecting the wishes and prejudices of the white soldiers about them. The full loss of the Cheyennes was never determined until their surrender at Red Cloud Agency, Dakota, a number of weeks after, when they submitted a list of forty killed, but never stated the number of wounded, either on account of superstition or some undefined repugnance to dwelling upon the topic.

Not the battle-field alone was unkind to them. From the desperate cold of the night immediately following they suffered as much. Eleven little babies froze to death in the arms of famished mothers, and ponies had to be killed that feeble old men and women might prolong their lives by inserting feet and legs in the warm entrails. This night was of unusual severity: the spirit-thermometers in our supply camp registered almost, although not quite, 30° below zero. These facts were not learned, as I say, for some time after the fight. I prefer to introduce them here to make the story more coherent. It was always a difficult matter to get any of them to speak of their frozen children, or to name their dead. (An American Indian will never, except under the pressure of a grave exigency, mention the name of his mother-in-law, or of a friend who has lately died.) The gashed legs and arms of mourning widows and orphan girls were about as good a sign as any one could demand of the extent of their loss and the depth of the grief it had provoked.

The destruction of the village would have been a veritable triumph for us, without the killing or wounding of a single Cheyenne. Never had so rich and complete a prize fallen into the hands of the Regular Army from the day of its first organization.

Two hundred lodges—nearly all of canvas, but a considerable percentage of buffalo hide—were, each and every one, a magazine of ammunition, fixed and loose, and a depot of supplies of every mentionable kind.

A few, not more than half a dozen at most, were of extra-large size, and filled with saddles and war-like trappings ranged round the circular floor; these were the convention halls or lodge rooms of the "soldier" societies: others, petty in dimensions, were allotted to women living in seclusion.

Not infrequently, artistic taste was evident in pictographs upon the hide or canvas walls; and where the head of a lodge was a person of importance, his shield, ornamented with his "totem," and "medicine," was suspended from a post or a tree-branch in front of the entrance.

Soldiers detailed upon a work of destruction have no time for indulgence in the contemplation of the aesthetic development of savages; a great task had been assigned us, and all that night and well into the next morning, Russell's troop of the 3d Cavalry and Davis' of the 4th toiled and burned, wiping off the face of the earth many products of aboriginal taste and industry which would have been gems in the cabinets of museums.

First, all the fat and marrow preserved by the squaws in great bladders and paunches were laid upon the lodge-fires, upon which were then piled the cords and cords of fuel gathered as the winter supply. The crackling flames roared and bellowed in their skyward rush through the covering of hide and canvas, but before the lodge-poles could fairly ignite, the explosion of kegs and cans of powder sent all the belongings of Cheyenne domestic life rocket-like to the zenith.

Never were orders more thoroughly executed. Experience had taught us in bitter lessons the preceding winter that villages only half destroyed were scarcely to be considered injured at all, and on this occasion the determination was to let not one square inch of canvas, of hide, of robe, or even of gunny sack be available for future use by the discomfited enemy.

Lodge-poles, not more than half burned, were broken into smaller fragments and thrown upon what it is no rhetorical flourish to call the funeral pyres of Cheyenne glory. Axes, spades, picks, shovels, hammers, scissors and knives were burned to deprive them of their temper: holes were knocked in the bottom of canteens, kettles, pans and all other utensils, before subjecting them to heat; saddles were smashed, bridle-reins cut, bits broken, and then thrown to the conflagration.

Many weapons of excellent make were seized and these were exempt from the common fate. Seven hundred head of stock fell into our hands, not quite one hundred of the number being loaded by our Pawnees with such plunder as appealed to their fancy.

How many tons of buffalo-meat were consumed, I couldn't pretend to say; when we took possession of the village we found immense stacks of it aggregating thousands of pounds and sufficient to last the enemy until spring; we didn't stop to estimate its amount, but promptly tossed it in alongside of blazing saddles and steaming fat, to add its quota of crackling noise to the detonation of bursting ammunition.

That this band of Cheyennes had been in the very thick of the fight with Custer* was evident to the least discerning and increased the zeal which pressed us in our exertions.

*The Battle of the Little Bighorn, June 25, 1876.—Ed. 2015

As we watched the untanned buffalo skins, the robes and blankets baking to a crisp; or threw in alongside of them bottles of strychnine used by the Cheyennes to poison wolves, or bullet moulds and empty cartridge shells, useless to us, but priceless at this time to the enemy, there fell at our feet all the Lares and Penates of primitive man, with a liberal contribution of much that the taste of civilization could devise or its art and industry fabricate.

First, let me enumerate the principal features of the evidence implicating this particular band in the Custer Massacre.

Memorandum books of the First Sergeants of the 7th Cavalry; one of these had in it an entry made the very day of the massacre: "Left Rosebud June 25th." This had subsequently been used by a Cheyenne warrior to contain the picture-history of his own prowess. On one page, he was to be seen murdering a poor teamster; on the next, he was killing a wretched miner. At one point, he was running away from [Major Marcus] Reno's barricade on the hill (represented by a round line of fire, with saddled horses lying down inside), amid a hurricane of bullets; in this rencontre, the Cheyenne represented himself wounded once and his horse four times.

Cavalry horses branded U. S. and 7C.

Saddles, canteens, nose-bags, curry-combs, brushes, rosters of companies, shovels and axes—all marked with the letter of the company in the 7th Cavalry, to which they had belonged.

A book containing the names of the three best shots at each target-practice of Captain Donald McIntosh's company, 7th Cavalry.

Donald McIntosh, of mixed Caucasian and Native American ancestry, died in the initial fight in the Little Bighorn Valley during the retreat to the bluffs led by Major Reno.—Ed. 2015

An officer's blue Mackintosh cape.

A buckskin jacket, lined with taffeta, supposed from its marks and appearance to have been worn on the fatal day by Captain Tom Custer.

Killed with General Custer were two of his brothers, Tom and Boston, his 17-year-old nephew Autie Reed, and his brother-in-law, James Calhoun.—Ed. 2015

A gold pencil-case.

A silver watch.

Pocket-books, containing currency and coin. "Sharp Nose," the Arapahoe chief, in rummaging about in the tents, was the delighted discoverer of a wad of greenbacks containing not quite fifty dollars.

The hat of Sergeant William Allen, company "I," 3d Cavalry, killed in the fight of June 17th, 1876, with Crook's forces. (Identified by name on the band.)

Letters received from relatives at home and letters written and ready to be mailed; one to a young lady in the East had a stamp on it and everything ready for mailing.

Photographs, one of which I pasted in my note-book, where it still is. Among these, were also found: A full cartridge belt, with a silver plate, marked "Little Wolf," presented to this Indian when he was visiting Washington. This was taken from the body of a dead warrior to whom "Little Wolf" had given it, or who had won it from "Little Wolf," in gambling.

The scalps of two young girls, neither of full age; one a flaxen-haired Caucasian; the other, a Shoshonee.

A buckskin bag containing the right hands of twelve Shoshonee babies.

The hand and arm of a Shoshonee squaw.

The scalp of the Shoshonee warrior killed on our side at the Rosebud, June 17th; recognized by his friends by the ornaments in the hair.

A necklace of human fingers. This ghastly specimen of aboriginal religious art, the especial "medicine" decoration of "High Wolf," the chief "medicine-man," can be inspected at the National Museum, Washington, D. C., where it was deposited by me last year.

Scalp shirts, fringed with human hair, savage and civilized.

War bonnets of eagle feathers.

Shields.

And many other specimens of dress, art and manufactures.

Many of the squaw's robes of delicately tanned antelope skin, encrusted with bead-work, or stained porcupine quills, or glistening with the nacreous lustre of elk teeth, were marvels of beauty.

The Cheyennes were not unmindful of the creature comforts. Plates, cups and saucers of china-ware; spoons, knives, forks, scissors, coffee-pots, pillows, even mattresses, showed that the presence of the white man was beginning to develop new wants, excite new appetites. Alongside of these, were the primitive forms of implements—stone hammers and fruit and nut mashers for making the palatable compound known to the Sioux as "Toro," in which powdered buffalo meat, wild plums, and, occasionally, wild cherries, are beaten to a pulp and incorporated with boiling marrow: stone pipes, sometimes inlaid with silver, and at other times without ornament, but always accompanied by tobacco-bags, most elaborately ornamented with bead and quill work.

There was little sleep for our people throughout that cold, frosty night; the Shoshonees, half-crazy with grief, gave full rein to their sorrow in weeping and singing, weirdly monotonous, but deeply impressive.

They reasoned, and subsequent events proved they reasoned wisely, that the Cheyennes had just returned from the destruction of one of the outlying villages of their tribe, in some exposed position in the Wind River range, and that we had been listening to the savage dance which celebrated this fearful butchery. All sympathy was rejected; they surrendered themselves to the most abject grief, and letting their hair hang down over face and shoulders, danced and wailed, and wailed and danced until darkness had passed away, neglecting to assume the new battle-names which the Pawnees alongside of them adopted, according to the usage of the Plains tribes, with much smoking and other ceremonial.

There was no shooting into our lines during the night, and when morning dawned on the 26th, no enemy was in sight, but a reconnaissance made by our Indian scouts developed them in a strong position six miles distant. No hostile demonstrations were exchanged and the day passed without incident.

Another dead Cheyenne was found in the rocks, and four other dead ponies were come upon, killed by our fire, and the skeletons of six butchered by the starving Cheyennes for food.

The column was ordered to saddle and move back to rejoin the infantry. As the march was taken up it began to snow heavily. Two or three Cheyennes entered their ruined village almost the moment our men had withdrawn and sat down and bewailed the spectacle of their desolated home. They were not molested. They were, of course, not a bit more afflicted than the others of their tribe, but possibly represented them all. Examples of just such Ceremonial Weeping I have seen at the Rosebud, at the Sun Dance and elsewhere. It was an observance known to the Hebrews, who, "by the waters of Babylon" "sat down and wept," and to other nations. We marched not more than twelve miles, the day being very cold, and our wounded needing careful attention. The bodies of our dead, frozen hard, were slung over the backs of pack-mules, which at first were restive and frightened, but by the end of an hour or so became reconciled to their ghastly cargoes.

The wounded were our greatest care. Lodge-poles, reserved from the destruction of the village, were arranged one on each side of an aparejo, the ends trailing on the ground, and blankets or gunny-sacks made fast in the manner of a cot or litter, in which the patient was placed, warmly wrapped, and thus dragged along the frozen soil.

The route became very slippery from the impress of hundreds of hoofs; and, where intersected by deep ravines, almost impassable for these "travois." In one particularly bad place the frightened mules had to be pushed over the edge of the declivity, and allowed to slide down, sustained by stout ropes held by the enlisted men, and the ends of the "travois" supported in like manner.

And when we reached Willow Creek, which we crossed before going into camp on the other side, the extremities of the "travois" poles were secured in the bight of a rope, held by men on horseback riding alongside.

The beneficial effect of "travois" travelling upon the health of wounded men, is due, it seems to me, to the absence of jolting and the fact that, in every position the sick man's head is higher than the body.

A detachment of our Pawnees and Shoshonees who had gone on a reconnaissance to develop the enemy's position, and, if possible, determine his intentions, rejoined us during the day. They succeeded in getting in upon the remnant of the Cheyenne herd and were making off with over one hundred ponies, when their presence was discovered, and had it not been for the providential interposition of a dense snow-storm, their lives would have paid forfeit for their temerity. They escaped with a few of the ponies and the information, highly appreciated by us, that the Cheyennes seemed badly cut up, almost naked, without blankets, moccasins or ammunition, and hauling many wounded in the direction of the head of Crazy Woman's Fork of the Powder.

There was a wounded Shoshonee—"Anzi," by name—shot through the intestines and marked, so our surgeons said, for death. It was really no use trying to save him and all that could be done was to give him as much whiskey as he wanted, with a trifle of morphia.

Anzi's thirst for whiskey was very much like a New York alderman's thirst for "boodle;" the more he got the more he wanted. The medical panniers were emptied for him and the last drop poured into his mouth, to his inexpressible pleasure; but finding that no more was to come, with many an imprecation upon the "Mellican Medicine-man," he rolled out of his "travois" and was assisted to the back of a pony which he rode all day. He basely went back on the doctors' predictions, returned with his people across the mountains, nearly two hundred miles of travel, and when I saw him at Fort Washakie, during the Nez Perce campaign in the following year, he was still living, although by no means, so his friends told me, the man he had been before being so terribly wounded.

The remainder of the march back to the supply camp was almost featureless. One of our wounded men, a brave soldier named McFarland, died on the 28th of November, and the same day we had to face another rather stiff snow-storm with the usual polar breeze.

General Crook, with Colonels Dodge and Townsend with the infantry and artillery, had made a forced march to join us, overcoming every obstacle of cutting wind, driving snow and frozen trail, marching night and day continuously until the head of our column was sighted when they took the back-trail to the supply-camp.

The Commanding General's telegram to the War Department announcing Mackenzie's fight contains the following paragraph: "I can't commend too highly his brilliant achievements and the gallantry of the troops of his command. This will be a terrible blow to the hostiles, as those Cheyennes were not only their bravest warriors but have been the head and front of most all the raids and deviltry committed in this country."

A reply to this reached us in a few days, [General Phil] Sheridan saying: "It gives me great pleasure to transmit to you the following dispatch from the General of the Army [William Tecumseh Sherman], to which I add my own congratulations." And Sherman to Sheridan: "Please convey to Generals Crook and Mackenzie my congratulations, and assure them that we appreciate highly the services of our brave officers and men who are now fighting savages in the most inhospitable regions of our continent. I hope their efforts this winter will result in perfect success and that our troops will hereafter be spared the necessity of these hard winter campaigns."

Thanksgiving Day, November 30th, 1876, was devoted to the mortuary services of all our dead, excepting Lieutenant McKinney, whose body, enclosed in a pine box, was forwarded under charge of Lieut. O. L. Wieting, 23d Infantry, to Memphis, Tenn.

The graves were excavated on the summit of a low terrace and arranged side by side.

There was no gorgeous ritual, no solemn chant, no peal of cathedral organ or sad refrain of cathedral bell, but more tenderly imposing than all these was the funeral procession of over six hundred weather-beaten veterans, headed by Generals George Crook, Ranald Mackenzie, Colonels Dodge, Townsend and Gordon, with the members of their Staffs, and the hundreds of savage auxiliaries—which moved with measured tread to the place of sepulture and there halted until the extracts from the Book of Common Prayer had been read.

The usual funeral salute was fired, and then the bugles sang "taps" and our heroes were left to sleep their last sleep undisturbed.

The expedition next worked its way down to the Belle Fourche and the country at the extreme head of the Little Missouri. On the 1st of December, Sergeant Patterson of Captain Hemphill's company, 4th Cavalry, was killed by having his horse slip under him on the icy ground, the shock rupturing a blood vessel inside the Sergeant's body, producing instant death.

On the 3d of that month, our Shoshonee guides after full consultation with General Crook, made up their minds to return home and look after their people, being still apprehensive that some great disaster had overtaken one of their villages, as proved afterwards to have been the case. Our parting with them was such as would take place between brothers bound together by the ties of dangers conquered and elements defied together.

The wounded and sick, with the horses that had begun to play out were ordered back to Fort Fetterman, under command of Colonel

Gordon, an officer whose memory will not fade among his comrades so long as gallantry shall be held in honor, or genial wit and good-fellowship be looked upon as worthy qualities in a soldier.

It is hardly worthwhile to repeat scenes of distress and discomfort; my readers must by this time have come to the conclusion that we were not on a summer picnic. Almost every day a fierce blizzard paid us its respects, and nearly every night saw us bivouac in some spot where water was scarce, alkaline and muddy; fuel scanty and poor; in fact, but grease-wood and sage-brush. At the rise of the "Little Powder" we had to use water from a "water-hole" swarming with wriggling worms. We boiled the fluid but made as little use of it as possible, fearing results such as happen in Guinea, under the same circumstances.

Of food for our men there was no lack; the pack-trains carried a sufficiency of rations, and back with the wagons more ample supplies were always to be had. The occasion of anxiety was the forage for the animals; even with every wounded man and every broken-down horse culled out, and one hundred Shoshonees ordered back to their homes, there were needed thirty thousand pounds of grain per diem, and grain we had to have, the ground being mantled with snow, and grass not always accessible. 500,000 pounds had been accumulated at Fetterman, as much at Reno, and 300,000 pounds every fortnight were to move from the railroad to Fetterman, there to await such orders as might be sent in, but the dispatches received about December 10th from Colonel Carleton, 3d Cavalry, commanding Fort Fetterman, were decidedly discouraging. The severe storms of snow and wind had blockaded the Union Pacific Railroad, choked up "Medicine Bow" Gap, and made travel for wagons almost an impossibility. The companies of cavalry left at Fetterman had been dismounted and the horses put in carts, wagons and every kind of wheeled vehicle to hurry forage to the front, and yet the supply was inadequate, and it seemed as if many of our poor horses were fated to pave with their bones the trail we had followed.

The human beings had no cause to complain; my notes record that on December 9th no less than seventy-five elk, deer, antelope and big jackass rabbits were killed—and there are occasional references to porcupine—altogether enough to make a toothsome addition to the components of the army ration.

Frank Gruard, our chief scout, Ben Rowland and others, helped me as much as possible in getting together vocabularies of the Arapahoe, Cheyenne, Pawnee and Sioux languages.

I was not ignorant enough to give the slightest credit to the sensational story set afloat by Burton, the English traveller, to the effect that the Arapahoe dialect was so meagre that for purposes of conversation the members of that tribe had to rely upon the "Sign Language." This statement had been quoted by E. B. Tyler in his *Early History of Mankind*, a work I had with me, and it was therefore proper to verify or refute it. It took a very small examination to satisfy me that the Arapahoe tongue was copious, and, if deprived of its guttural and nasal modulation, would not be without beauty and softness.

The Cheyennes followed upon our trail and made two attacks upon careless parties of miners; in the first instance, no harm was done, but in the other, the results were very serious. There were eleven miners, who feeling a false security from being so near our camp, concluded to go to sleep without posting sentinels, at the coal-measure where Major Furey had had his blacksmiths at work during the day shoeing the mules of the wagon train. The attacking party of five Cheyennes was bold in its onslaught. A volley was poured in among the sleeping miners, none of whom was hurt, with the exception of one brained with his own axe. All the horses, blankets, guns, ammunition and provisions left behind by the miners in their flight fell into the hands of the Cheyennes.

Information reached camp shortly before midnight; a squad of Pawnee scouts was dispatched at once, but, beyond developing the above facts, was unsuccessful in pursuit. The Cheyennes had broken into small fragments, the better to obtain food in the chase, and also the more successfully to elude pursuit. Whether it was the party just spoken of or some other, I can't say, but we were informed a few weeks after at Red Cloud Agency that a couple of the Cheyennes had crept up to within ear-shot of one of our camp-fires and satisfied themselves that we really had a good-sized detachment of their own people among our auxiliaries; during the fight they refused to believe that there were any Cheyennes on our side save Bill Roland and maybe two or three half-breeds. This was the last straw; they saw that further resistance would be useless and acted upon their convictions by surrendering at Red Cloud Agency. On the 20th of December the very unwelcome news came from General Sheridan that our expenses for "transportation," etc., had exceeded a monthly average of $60,000, while the appropriations would not admit of more than $28,000 being spent. This was tantamount to an order to abandon the campaign. Our horses and mules were doing their best on half-rations, but couldn't do that very long if we were not to be able to hire transportation to supply them with food. The expedition was at that time on the Belle Fourche, on the N. W. corner of the Black Hills; from that point, it slowly worked its way back to Fetterman, there to disband until the advent of spring should enable the animals to derive some nutriment from the grass.

Antelope and elk were seen at intervals and some brought down. The Indians imparted their ideas on the subject of cookery. A few of their dishes are not by any means unpalatable. An elk heart, boiled in salt water is good enough for anybody. Antelope liver, sliced thin, laid on hot embers until done on both sides, is extremely appetizing. A deer or antelope head, roasted in the ashes, is toothsome, and some of the preparations of buffalo entrails, cooked in the same manner (which, however, we had eaten during the preceding summer and winter, and not on this expedition) were savory and palatable. My scientific enthusiasm did not sustain me to the pitch of trying the half-melted liver of an elk which had been chased over half a county and upon which liver there had been sprinkled a pinch of gall: I couldn't try that, but I did share in a handful of elk-liver, fresh from the animal, and found it to taste very much like a raw oyster. Despite the arctic temperature, which began to tell on the mules and horses, some of which would be found stiff and glassy-eyed each morning, and upon officers and men, among whom the surgeons found sufficient employment for their leisure moments in treating frozen feet, hands, ears and noses, the Indian scouts, constrained by a sense of duty which didn't allow them to wait for an invitation, gave the camp a serenade almost every night. First, the

Sioux serenaded the Pawnees, danced for them and made presents of horses; the next night the Pawnees sang, danced and gave the old crow-baits back. Ditto, the whole business for the Arapahoes; ditto for the Cheyennes. Then the Arapahoes, fired by enthusiasm, went over the whole programme with the Sioux and we had to endure another round of dittoes. Nobody growled about that; we were assured it was a ceremonial observance among our aboriginal friends and having been paid to cheerfully suffer all such little privations, we made the best face we could over the matter and smiled through our tears.

It took us very little time to discover that the gentle savage is as full of tricks as Adelina Patti.*

*Adelina Patti (1843–1919) was a highly acclaimed Italian opera singer.—Ed. 2015

Just as we were getting ready for a real good honest sleep, the Pawnees started in on a Farewell Tour; the Sioux, not to be outdone, and "in deference to the urgent request of many patrons, kindly consented to appear for this night only;" and the Arapahoes "yielding to the importunate demands of a clamorous public had cancelled important European engagements in order to, etc., etc., etc." We managed to live through it all. It was a very gloomy season in our lives, one I would gladly bury in oblivion.

Judge of my feelings when I say that one of the first things I was asked in Washington was to write a treatise on Indian music!

The weather grew colder and colder. To save our animals as much as possible they were not tied up at night, but allowed to run round unrestrained for the double purpose of keeping themselves warm under the shelter of friendly knolls, and of getting such nibbles of grass as might be found in sheltered spots not covered by snow. Wherever we could provide it, cottonwood foliage was fed to the mules; it is bitter, but not unpalatable, and much used by the Indians for their ponies in winter.

The sharp cold air of these winter mornings had the effect of intensifying the profane powers of our packers and teamsters whose language is quite often as amusing from its originality as it is shocking in its blasphemy and irreverence.

Whack! goes the whip, and—!—!—! comes a torrent of objurgation from the irate mule-drivers. The mule's long ears catch the stream of unsanctified music floating through the air which warns him that "business" is meant. So he begins to tug in dead earnest on the traces, and with the encouragement of another crack or two from the "black-snake," and another string of expletives, succeeds, with the help of his comrades, in pulling the wagon through the mud-hole or snow-drift in which it has mired.

This is an outline description of their behavior under ordinary circumstances. In the presence of graver difficulties, they become appalled and not even the encomiums of the mule-drivers can induce them to advance one foot before the other.

Suppose the wagon at the foot of a steep acclivity, the ground incrusted with ice or frozen snow. The "leaders" look upward and see the case is hopeless. They consult with each other. Mules are the greatest animals in the world for consulting together, and when the driver of a team sees his animals turning their heads towards each other and about to begin a conference, he at once abandons the struggle in despair, altho' he usually cracks his whip half a dozen times and explodes in a volley of objurgation, by way of dignified retreat. The next step is to send for the pioneer party which loses no time in breaking into the sandy ground, frozen hard as flint by the inclement winds. After a footing has been picked out and dug out for the mules, long ropes are attached to the wagon-tongue, and strong hands take hold and pull, while hands equi-strong seize upon axle and wagon-body and push with might and main.

The mules may still refuse to stir a hoof; the genuine army mule loves to be coaxed, and if the driver be not a fraud now is the opportunity to demonstrate that his wages have not been paid him in vain. "Whoop! Whoop-la! Gee! Gee! You Puss-mules! You Billy! Damn you, Billy! You—! —! —Billy! Dick! You Keno!"

The men whoop and yell and cheer and push and pull. All at once, the mules make a simultaneous effort and jerk the wagon up the grade on a run. Then the teamster licks his mules, just for luck; the wagon-master damns the teamster, the quartermaster damns the wagon-master and the pioneer party damn the quartermaster. But the team has surmounted its last difficulty before reaching camp for the night, and the voices of the mules are now upraised in a song of gladness. Much objection has been made to this chanting, as practised by mules, but the objection strikes me as frivolous and untenable. The mule's song may be just a particle monotonous and the nasal pitch he commonly employs, somewhat harsh for cultivated ears, but the question of pitch is a question of taste, and the mule's taste may be better than our own; or, if worse, this is the land of liberty, and the mule is free to enjoy himself as he pleases.

The charge of monotony is true, but it applies with equal force to the song of the lark, we all pretend to admire. We may admit the mule's lack of taste and skill in the rendition of his scanty repertoire, but we cannot deny him a full meed of praise for the earnestness with which he throws his whole soul into his work and pours forth his voice in song.

The pack-trains have frequently received my favorable notice in these pages. I can only add to what has already been said, that in winter as in summer and spring, our packers, under the able supervision of Tom Moore, attended with an assiduity almost devotion to the wants of the animals under their care. Some of them were droll fellows; all of them far above the average in intelligence, or above what their rough garb and unshaved faces would lead an observer to imagine. Seated by the camp-fire by night, I often listened to their conversation and never failed to be impressed with the clearness and accuracy of their judgment.

While on the Belle Fourche, one of them came up to see me. He was considerably under the influence of Black Hills whiskey brought in by parties from Deadwood. He began narrating his "up and downs," or more strictly speaking, his unchanging "downs" in the world. He had been a private soldier in the 4th Infantry before the War, at the period when Grant, Sheridan, Kautz, Stanley, Hood and Augur were captains and lieutenants in that regiment: "and now," he said, musingly, "they've every last one of them been made a gineral;

'n who'm I? Nobody. I never was nobody. I never expect to be nobody. The highest I ever got to be in the world was a lance-corporal's bunkey."

Slowly we progressed southward to the line of the North Platte, the days becoming colder and colder, the nights more and more dismal: to keep one's head out from under the protection of buffalo robes meant frozen ears and nose; to keep it under threatened suffocation.

There was about the winter scenery of that part of Wyoming a bleak and barren dreariness, whose monotony at times appalled the traveller conscious of its magnitude.

Mile succeeded mile as the column advanced, but no change occurred in the perspective of snow-mantled hillocks, gashed with ravines and tufted on their summits with a scanty line of timber. The leaden pall of the cloudy sky was an effective setting for the cheerless landscape which, in spite of its gloom, had still a weird fascination over the sight which never tired of looking at it.

The winding courses of the streams were defined by the skeleton limbs of trees, whence every bird had flown. Even crows and such carrion eaters were seen only at intervals, but once or twice the honk-honking of wild geese, high in air, announced a migration of those birds to the South.

One of the most disagreeable days in my experience was Christmas, 1876. We were pushing across the Pumpkin Buttes, doing our best to get into bivouac and escape the fury of the elements, which seemed eager to devour us. Beards, moustaches, eye-lashes and eye-brows were frozen masses of ice. The keen air was filled with minute crystals, each cutting the tender skin like a razor, while feet and hands ached as if beaten with clubs. Horses and mules shivered while they stood in column, their flanks white with crystals of perspiration congealed on their bodies, and their nostrils bristling with icicles.

Two of our thermometers indicated 26° below zero, Fahrenheit; neither was of any service. Spirit glasses in Deadwood registered that day 40° below, and in Fort Sanders, Wyoming, 58° below zero,

Fahrenheit, and we were in the direct line of the blast howling between those two points.

Major George M. Randall joined us with seventy-six Crow Indians, all that remained of over two hundred, who had started out from the Agency in the Judith Basin, Montana. Their march had been one of phenomenal severity: crossing the Yellowstone at the mouth of Clark's Fork, up that and the Big Rosebud to their heads, thence to the Gray Bull and Stinking Water, on to the Big Horn River, across it and the Big Horn Mountains to the source of the Tongue—down that a few miles, and then south to Cantonment Reno, and thence on our trail until they overtook us, returning at Pumpkin Buttes. Most of the Crows became thoroughly disheartened and declined to face the fearful inclemency of the weather. Randall and his interpreter, Fox, endeavored without avail to persuade them to continue. The greater number returned to the Agency, spreading the report that Randall and their comrades had been frozen to death in a snow-storm in the Big Horn Mountains. This had almost been the case. In the worst of the storm Randall's people discovered that they were in the midst of a small herd of buffalo, and began shooting right and left. The warm carcasses furnished protection to the nearly frozen feet and legs, which were thrust into them, and raw steaks devoured greedily by famished stomachs that had eaten nothing for more than two days.

When within less than fifty miles of Fetterman, we found waiting for us Louis Richaud, a half-breed Frenchman and more than two hundred scouts, from the Spotted Tail Agency. The change in the programme sent them back, slightly in advance of the expedition, their horses being in prime condition.

The impossibility of procuring anything like a sufficiency of forage for the cavalry, compelled the expedition to march to Fort Laramie and other points, to be put in good condition for the earliest days of spring. But the Spring campaign was not to be. There remained but one band of any size, in spirit to fight, on the American side of the British Line—the band of "Crazy Horse," one of the foremost of the hostile Sioux chiefs. The Cheyennes were broken and humbled, and runners from them had arrived at Red Cloud Agency to say that they were coming in as fast as they could to surrender, and were so dissatisfied with the inhospitable reception granted them by "Crazy Horse" when they sought shelter in his camp after the fight of the 25th November that they would gladly go out to attack him with the American forces.

The game was in our hands, and, after the weary marching and countermarching of two winter campaigns, and one during the summer which for severity was almost Hobson's choice—after fighting the enemy on the lower Powder, Montana, in February and March; on the Tongue River, Wyoming, and on the Rosebud, Montana, in June; on Goose Creek, Wyoming, in July; at Slim Buttes, Dakota, in September, and on Willow Creek, in November, we had the gratification of receiving messengers begging the Government to stay its hand, and give all those on the war-path a chance to collect their wives and families and bring them to the Reservation.

"Spotted Tail," one of the shrewdest of the American aborigines, frankly admitted that further resistance on the part of the hostiles would be suicide and not warfare; twelve months previously, his sarcastic predictions of the dangers to befall the troops had proved him to be at least a sympathizer with those of his tribe arrayed against the Government.

But for reasons not necessary to recapitulate he was at this period most anxious to be individually the means of bringing in "Crazy Horse," and thus solidifying his position in the tribe and with the Government.

After submitting his proposition to General Crook, and having conferred fully with Colonel Julius W. Mason, 3rd Cavalry, commanding the troops on his Reservation, he started out to see "Crazy Horse," and had no difficulty in letting that stubborn redskin understand that he must come in on the full run.

There would be the same, and possibly a larger force of white soldiery to fight when the snow melted, there was no help to be expected from the Reservations, which were under strict surveillance and, worst feature of all, was the certainty that more than one thousand Indian scouts, regularly enlisted or going along as free-lances, would obey the orders of the Government when the movement began.

So, first the Cheyennes, under "Dull Knife" and "Little Wolf," surrendered, making but one condition, that they be allowed to send their warriors with the white soldiers to fight "Crazy Horse; and lastly, "Crazy Horse" himself and his band.

The aggregate of men, women and children thus surrendering at "Red Cloud" and "Spotted Tail" agencies, was not quite four thousand five hundred, but of the ponies, which ran up into the thousands, I failed to keep a complete record. "Crazy-Horse's" people alone had more than two thousand.

My relations with these people, either in Peace or War, did not terminate here, but the expedition did and so must my story which, disconnected and hastily prepared as it is, will still, I hope, give my readers a good, general idea of the manner in which our expeditions were conducted against the savage tribes in the unknown region which has within the past winter supplied our national standard with the beautiful stars of the two Dakotas and Montana, and will soon, I trust, add still another for Wyoming.

THE END

BIG BYTE BOOKS is your source for great lost history!

Printed in Great Britain
by Amazon